How to ATTRACT ATTENTION with your ART

A Guide for Graphic Artists

IVAN TUBAU

STERLING PUBLISHING CO., INC. NEW YORK

Oak Tree Press Co., Ltd.
Distributed by WARD LOCK, Ltd., London & Sydney

OTHER BOOKS OF INTEREST

Abstract Art
Acrylic and Other Water-Base Paints
Color in Oil Painting
Complete Crayon Book
Composition in Art
Drawing from Nature

Experiments in Modern Art
Express Yourself in Drawing
Freehand Lettering
Landscape Drawing with Pencil
Painting Abstract Landscapes
Postercraft

Translated by Jennifer Mellen

Copyright © 1970 by
Sterling Publishing Co., Inc.
419 Park Avenue South, New York, N.Y. 10016
British edition published by Oak Tree Press Co., Ltd.
Distributed in Great Britain and the Commonwealth by
Ward Lock, Ltd., 116 Baker Street, London W1
The original edition was published in Spain under the title
"Diseño Publicitario" © 1969 by Santillana, S. A. de Ediciones, Madrid
Manufactured in the United States of America
All rights reserved
Library of Congress Catalog Card No.: 79-126846
ISBN 0-8069-5154-0   UK 7061 2258 5
5155-9

Contents

1. The Visual Arts

If you refer to a dictionary in search of the meaning of the word art, you would find an explanation that would sound something like this: "Creative human activity that, with no practical objective, attempts to represent the experiences of a community or an individual, and give sensitive expression to the supersensory."

The encyclopedia will also tell you that art embraces Poetry—with a capital letter—Music, Painting, Architecture and Sculpture (which, seemingly for purposes of classification, are considered one and the same thing), Dance and the Theatre.

In effect, it occurred to someone, many centuries ago, to determine that the arts total six. But to us, in these last decades of the twentieth century, such a classification is too brief.

During the Middle Ages—and much before that in China—*xylography*, or wood engraving, was in use. Can the engraving be considered a *painting*? It seems to us that, technically, it cannot. But in the past century and in this century, too, things have become even more complicated. The cinema appeared; after much discussion of whether or not it constituted a new art form, some admirers of classical culture decided to label it the *seventh art*.

But, what of television? And photography? Are they not art? Surely they are, or at least they can be. What number should we assign to them?

The best solution would be to renounce any attempt to classify from the beginning, and limit ourselves to those arts that from the point of view of this book interest us: the *visual arts*.

With this in mind, we discard music—which reaches us through the ear—and literature, which appeals more to the understanding than to the eye. We also discard those forms of the visual arts involving *movement*—theatre, dance, movies, animated drawings—and *solid three-dimensional forms*: architecture, sculpture.

We have now reduced the field substantially, haven't we? In effect, we have simplified the question: of the six classical arts we are left with one: painting.

Painting and Drawing

Painting—to continue to use the encyclopedia's definition—is that branch of art which, through lines and colors, represents on a surface the conceptions of the artist.

Now we have the principle: to paint is to place strokes or shapes—lines or colors—on a plane surface: cloth, wood, stone, metal. . . . In our case, principally *paper*.

For us, *drawing* will constitute all that is black on white, according to the "penline" technique that is the most used in commercial art, that sector of the visual arts which makes a business of attracting attention. As we will see at the proper time—very soon—in this technique we can use tools other than the pen.

Painting, for us, will be all that we prepare in color, whether the paint itself is gouache, oil, or cut-and-pasted papers. In drawing, *line* has enormous importance. In painting, it is *areas of color*.

What Is Advertising?

Let us not complicate our lives with trite definitions. Briefly, one could say that advertising is the art or the technique—some even go so far as to say the *science*—of *announcing* something.

At first glance it seems that "to announce" means, automatically, *announce to sell*. And, in effect, the vast majority of advertisements try to sell something: a product (sodas, dresses, foodstuffs), or a service (airline trips, spectaculars, lessons).

But advertising can have other objectives and possibilities: to disseminate ideas, for example, although ideological publicity is generally called *propaganda*.

A striking billboard

Graphic directions

Advertising can be:

■ *private*, when it advertises merchandise of a specific brand

■ *collective*, when it advertises a generic product, without a brand name (fish, wine, milk)

■ *municipal*, when it advertises things of interest to a specific municipality

■ *provincial or regional*, when what is being advertised is of interest to a particular province or region

■ *national*

■ *international* (worldwide anti-hunger drive)

To accomplish any of these goals, advertising may use many diverse media: radio, television, the cinema, the press, display windows, city walls or billboards in the country, brochures, or packaging.

All this forms part of *commercial art*. But we, to understand one another, will confine ourselves in the use of this term to *graphic* mediums, those that use the stationary image.

Graphic Art

Is advertising art? We will not enter again the forest of definitions. Of course, if we accepted that art is that which "has no practical objective," advertising would not be art, since it always has a practical goal: to sell or announce something.

But we should not assume that something ceases to be art simply because it has a practical goal, or because it serves something else. A painting, because it is a painting, is not in principle greater than a poster that advertises a theatrical spectacular.

But granted, there are both good and bad posters. One of Toulouse-Lautrec's posters announcing singer Jane Avril will always be superior to thousands and thousands of mediocre oil paintings filled with pretension.

An attractive
theatrical
poster by
Dudley
Hardy

It is clear, then, for us: the art of walls, newspapers and packaging is as valid as the art of museums. The artistic importance of a work depends upon its quality, not upon its purpose. A good *graphic artist*—which is what the professional utilitarian artist calls himself—is as important as a good painter. And, of course, a good graphic artist is *always* high above any mediocre painter.

We should not feel inferior, therefore, if commercial art attracts us more than traditional art: a graphic artist has, in principle, nothing to envy a gallery painter for; neither economically nor artistically should he feel inferior to him.

It is obvious that a graphic artist often must submit to the wishes of the client being imposed upon him, and he may be thwarted in his freedom of creativity. But this is another topic. And the painter, too, frequently is obliged to suffer the pressures of the merchants of art and the caprices of the powerful who buy his paintings, whose tastes, consciously or not, he tries to cater to.

Painting and Drawing in Advertising

Painting and drawing have a wide application in advertising. In this book we will study, briefly, in a simple and elemental manner, their principal applications.

An exciting street poster

12

The bull on the ancient wall paintings of Altamira Cave, Spain, gives the artist inspiration for a cigarette pack.

To cultivate any of the specialties of graphic art in advertising it is appropriate for us to master essentially two techniques: the *pen*, for works in black and white; and *gouache*, for color work. And the first thing we will do in the immediate pages, before beginning to study the various specialites, is to acquaint ourselves with both techniques.

The graphic artist, at times, also uses other paints, or pencil: we will discuss this, but without forgetting that the major part of our graphic art works will be executed in *pen* or in the *gouache* technique.

The graphic commercial artist frequently uses techniques that have nothing to do with *drawing* or *painting*: self-adhesive letters of the alphabet, similar to the decals we knew in childhood; laminated colored paper to be cut and pasted, more or less as in simple collages; various adhesive forms, such as circles, rectangles and squares; photographs; and printed letters.

And finally, *creativity* is as important in graphic art as is *technique*. Creativity is that process which carries through from the search for an idea to its final execution. First and foremost, you must be creative and unusual, even unique, to attract attention with your art.

Pencil sketch

Wash drawing

Line drawing

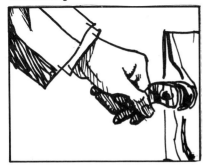

2. Line Drawing Techniques

The overwhelming majority of advertisements you see in the daily newspapers—and even many of those you see in magazines or brochures—are line drawings.

Not all of these drawings have been executed in the final stage with a pen. Many are done with a brush, some with a mechanical pen (which we will explain later on), others with a reed or even a grease pencil.

What do all these drawings have in common? They are all done in *black* and *white*—in *absolute* black and white: the white is completely white, the black completely black. There is no grey whatever.

At first glance some of these drawings seem to have grey zones. But if you look at them more carefully you will see that these apparent greys may in reality be formed by little *black* wiggles and waves or dots and lines, drawn *black* lines.

The pen only draws lines. Even solid shadows, in pen, must be patiently formed of lines. Unless you use red or grey or any other color ink, the lines of the pen will always be *black*.

India Ink

The one truly important element of this technique is the use of *undiluted India ink*. Any instrument, any working tool, dipped into this ink will produce drawings suitable for line engraving. That is, as long as white paper is used, of course.

What are the principal characteristics of this ink? For us, essentially two:

A balanced, suspenseful pen drawing with cross-hatch shading

No question about the focus of
attention in this advertisement

A clever way to picture broadcasting

1. IT IS ABSOLUTELY BLACK. Any ordinary black ink would do, in principle. But India ink offers the guarantee of a thick and total blackness, without the risk of greyed lines.

2. IT IS INDELIBLE. India ink cannot be erased with any known eraser. (We will explain later on how to correct errors when using India ink.) The fact that it is indelible also signifies that it cannot "run." If a drop of water falls on a drawing with ordinary ink, the ink will run, and the drawing will be ruined. With India ink, nothing will happen.

The major precaution to take with India ink is not to leave the bottle uncovered once you are through using it: if you do, the ink will *thicken*, making later use difficult. If it has thickened, you can thin it out with a little—a very little—drop of boiled water.

Papers

Always use white, of course. Inexpensive writing paper is not particularly suitable, because of its lack of consistency. It wrinkles as soon as you put on a large area of ink and it will be torn easily by the pen point. In some cases it gives off lint as the pen passes over it with any degree of force, in which case the drawing is ruined.

What is known as bond paper is somewhat better, although it is not always smooth and consistent enough. Certain other drawing papers *absorb* too much ink—they act like blotting papers—and therefore are unsuitable.

The best paper for India ink is known as Bristol. This is manufactured in various thicknesses (1-ply, 2-ply, etc.) by several companies. In general, any Bristol paper has enough body for pen drawings. All papers of this class are perfectly smooth on both sides.

For drawings in which you desire a slightly rougher line—especially when you use dry brush—use a kid finish paper which has a noticeable grain.

On kid finish paper, a rougher line

On Bristol board, a stronger line

Pencil and Eraser

The ordinary graphite pencil—the one commonly used to write or take notes—is only used in the "preparatory" phase of graphic art work, in the "sketch." Later on, when the drawing is completed in ink, the pencil is erased.

Pencil sketch partly inked in. Looking at people's backs is unusual enough to draw attention.

It is best to use quite a hard pencil for sketching. The soft pencils are marked B, the hard H. The higher the number the greater the degree of softness or hardness. For example, 5H is harder than 4H. Soft pencils give a dark line (the softest, 6B, black), while hard pencils give a grey line (very light in 9H, the hardest).

The most appropriate pencils for your work are 2H, or as soft as HB, which is at the middle of the hard-soft scale. Inexpensive pencils are numbered rather than lettered; No. 2 will serve your purposes perfectly.

Why not use soft pencils? Because they blacken and dirty the paper, confuse the sketch and make the job of erasing at the end more difficult.

You must always use the softest eraser possible, one that will be least likely to tear or wrinkle the paper. A kneaded rubber or an artist's gum eraser are best. It is not essential that they completely erase the pencil lines, since in reproduction by photoengraving and printing, the line cut will not reproduce pencil lines. When the drawing is printed, only the inked lines will be visible.

It is wise, even so, to wait until the ink is completely dry before erasing the pencil sketch lines. Otherwise, the eraser will blur the damp ink. At any rate, India ink dries quickly.

Rulers and Squares

You will seldom have to use straightedges in definitive ink drawings, since in general a freehand sketch is preferable. But they are useful in pencil sketches, to take exact measurements, to square corners, and to draw long straight lines that you will subsequently go over freehand.

We will not speak here of the use of the square and the ruler, since we suppose that you already know how to use these tools. We will say only that when you work on a sheet of paper already cut and squared by the manufacturer, you can measure the limits of your drawing, taking as a point of departure the borders of the paper. In case it is not square, you must square it off yourself.

The same with the compass: use it to draw circles in the preparatory phase, circles that only in some cases will you later trace over in ink using the compass.

City
buildings
drawn
with
pencil
and ruler,
then inked
in

Pens

For ink drawings use an artist's pen in a holder.

What distinguishes one pen point from another is its degree of *hardness* or *flexibility*. The hard ones do not "open" easily, and this allows you to draw very fine lines. The points of flexible pens separate easily, thus making possible both fine lines and broad ones, according to the pressure you apply.

There are many brands and numbers of pen points, especially artists' pens. The most important thing is to try as many pens as possible, until you discover the possibilities of each one and determine which is the best for your temperament, and your own style or method of drawing.

Clean your pen carefully with a cloth wiper upon finishing each job, as well as once in a while during your work, if it is prolonged. The point of the pen must not suffer blows, nor be "split" over the paper: it would become unusable.

The best method of protecting a pen while not being used is to deposit it in a jar or glass, with its point uppermost.

Frank Godwin effectively uses the pen exclusively

Brushes

You can draw the same lines with a brush as you can with a pen, if you know how to manipulate it. The brush requires a firmer control of the wrist, but once you know how to use it it gives a softer line than the pen (since it is more flexible) and it allows you to work faster.

Some of the best illustrators (Frank Godwin, for example) use the pen almost exclusively; others (Alex Raymond, for example) combine pen and brush; and not a few (Milton Caniff and Frank Robbins) work with brush exclusively.

But, apart from being used in the same manner as the pen (for lines) the brush has two other important applications: to fill in large areas of black, and to "cover up" mistakes with white opaque gouache.

We will speak of white opaque and the correction of mistakes later on. Regarding black areas, it is indisputable that the brush is much easier to use.

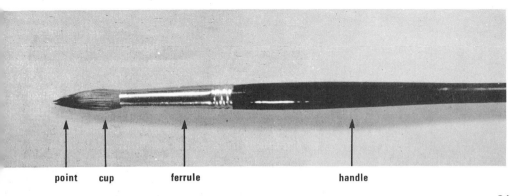

point   cup   ferrule   handle

After the pen line drawing is done, fill in black areas with a brush

Milton Caniff uses only a brush

To fill in a large black area with a pen, you must have patience, and join single lines until a mass is formed. Almost always this leads to "overloading" the area with ink. With the brush, filling-in is achieved better and faster, since the brush can hold plenty of ink and extend it across the paper evenly without forming stains. Of course, speed depends on the size of the brush.

There are flat and round brushes. For graphic art work, the round are most frequently used, although for certain thick and effective lines, you can use flat brushes.

Regarding the quality of the brush, the best are sable. When you buy a round brush, make sure that the bristles come to a perfect point. A "broomy" brush is unusable for drawing.

Regarding size, brushes carry numbers: the higher the number, the wider the brush. The most useful for drawing are the 4 or 6 for general work, the 2 for very fine lines, and the 10 or 12 to fill in black areas.

Do not press a brush vertically against the paper. Wash it carefully after use, with cold or warm water and soap, "combing" the hairs into a point. Store it with the brush uppermost, as you store your pens.

The brush may also be used damp, but we will speak of this later on.

Mechanical and India Ink Pens

Mechanical fountain pens (such as the Graphos, Rapidograph and Technos) with their various nibs are generally used for lettering and line drawings that will be reproduced. They are used like an ordinary drawing pen, but mostly for drawing straight lines that must be *uniform*, always even. For different thicknesses, you just need to change nibs. With them you can achieve excellent work, such as fine crossed lines or fine rulings. You must take the precaution of cleaning the point every so often with a cloth, to avoid ink stains.

The Graphos and Rapidograph are filled much like the ordinary fountain pen, but the Technos is filled with cartridges that are thrown away when empty.

23

2.5			0.8	
2.0			0.6	
			0.5	
1.7			0.4	
1.4			0.3	
1.2			0.2	
1.0			0.16	
			0.1	

The Technos pen and its changeable points

As for the points, the 0.1 is a tenth of a millimeter, and the 0.8 equals 8 millimeters. For us, the most appropriate are the 0.4 and the 0.6.

The great advantage of these pens is that they do not need to be dipped in a bottle regularly, since the ink flows evenly through the point, like a fountain pen. This permits uninterrupted, fast execution of a drawing, and the ability to work anywhere—on the street, in a restaurant, etc. The disadvantages of this tool are its extremely delicate mechanism (it clogs quite easily), and the invariable evenness of its line.

Reeds and Grease Pencils

A reed is, simply, a *reed*. It is a section of the stiff stem of a reed cut to a point. You dip it into ink just like any nib. It gives a "softer" line than the pen, but is less flexible than the brush. Its "rustic" line, very "artistic," can be used frequently in graphic art. Great artists like Cornet worked for newspapers using reeds almost exclusively. Similar effects can also be obtained with toothpicks—a simple toothpick or with any piece of wood dipped in ink.

The grease pencil is a very soft pencil that can draw on any surface, whether paper, glass, metal or lithographic stone. Since its black is quite intense, it can be used for drawings destined for linecut reproduction. This gives you a "wrinkled" style of drawing that resembles pencil.

Line and Wash

Describing the tools must have suggested to you different styles of drawings to experiment with.

Line and wash, the most frequent style in advertising art, has four subdivisions:

(a) Pure line
(b) Line shaded with line
(c) A combination of line and wash
(d) Pure wash.

A careful thinline drawing with cross-hatch shading

PURE LINE is the simplest style of all: it consists only of lines or silhouettes. There are no shadings whatever, nor solid blacks. Very delicate and elegant drawings can be achieved with this technique—and great beauty if the artist is good.

It was all done with a reed by Cornet

Various ways of using a pen to create straight lines with cross-hatches of wavy, twisted and curly lines to get shaded effects

Line shaded by line to create many middle or half tones.

Humorous line and wash poster by Heinz Edelmann

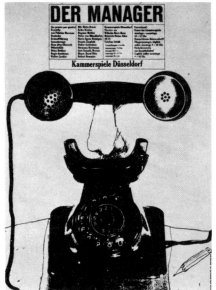

A simple well composed line and brush drawing

Varied Line is a pure line technique in which the thickness of the line varies: in some places it is fine, in others thick. If the line is to be even, mechanical fountain pens or the reed will serve; and if varied, a brush, flexible pen, grease pencil or reed can be used.

In works destined to be published, take care that your fine lines are not *too fine*. Since you will nearly always work in a size larger than the final drawing will be when published, and the thickness of your lines will be reduced photographically, the making of a line cut will "eat up" parts of your extremely fine lines.

Line Shaded by Line. With this technique, the shades are achieved through *cross-hatching*. These cross-hatches can be vertical, horizontal, fine, thick, straight, curved, twisted, dotted, close together or far apart.

Through the appropriate and correct combination of the different kinds of lines, you can achieve an almost unlimited range of shades.

Line and Wash. This is a technique appropriate for the brush, or the brush in combination with the other tools: pen, mechanical pen, reed. It is perhaps the technique most often used in commercial art—as well as illustration—since it permits a high grade of realism, great style, and ease of reproduction.

It consists simply of adding, over a line drawing, certain solid areas, particularly in the darkest parts, of absolute black. To fill in these zones, as we said previously, the fastest and most appropriate tool is a brush.

Pure Wash. This is an effective technique. There are no lines, simply solid blacks and clean whites, light and shade without intermediate shadings. This technique requires a careful pencil sketch in which all the problems of the drawing are resolved. Afterwards, you decide which areas should be black, and shade them with pencil.

Now all you have to do is cover the black zones with ink—using the brush or, if you want precisely defined limits, the pen. If you have marked the outlines of those areas with the brush, you should fill them in with the brush. And there it is: you erase the pencil and there appears a drawing without lines in which the figures or objects are "imagined" around the black washes.

In certain cases, it is wise perhaps to indicate with the pen some small detail without which it would not be possible to understand the drawing visually. At any rate, this is a difficult technique, which requires absolute control of the pen technique and a profound knowledge of drawing.

RUGGIERO RICCI

Kulturabteilung
Bayer Leverkusen
Erholungshaus

Konzert- und
Opernring 1966/67

Dienstag,
den 11. April 1967,
20.00 Uhr

Mittwoch,
den 12. April 1967,
20.00 Uhr

Bayer Philharmoniker   Ruggiero Ricci
Leitung: Erich Kraack   Violine

Werke:
Jean Sibelius,
3 Legenden

Peter Tschaikowsky,
Konzert für
Violine und Orchester
D-Dur op. 35

Anton Dvorák,
Slawische Tänze

Karten DM 2.- bis 6.-
Kulturabteilung,
Hauptkaufhaus und
Abendkasse

A pure wash poster for a German concert (Graphicteam). After the drawing was finished the large white type was "dropped out" photographically.

Pen over Pencil Style

This is an extremely difficult technique, which demands all your artistic command and patience. It consists of drawing in pen a series of parallel lines—fine lines in the light areas and progressively thicker in the zones in which the shade increases—until you have achieved a relief effect.

First, a careful pencil drawing must be executed, in which the zones of light and shade are perfectly valued. Then, you cover the entire drawing with parallel lines in pencil. Now you need only cover these lines in ink, *thickening* the lines by pressing hard on a flexible pen in the zones of shade, and *thinning* the lines (with very light pressure) in the light zones. Naturally, you do not want simply two thicknesses of lines, but a great variety of intermediate thicknesses between thin and thick.

The four steps in
drawing pen over
pencil. If you have
the patience to
draw this way,
you will surely
attract attention.

Fiat 693N1

Striking advertisement in the
pen over pencil technique

Fiat 650E

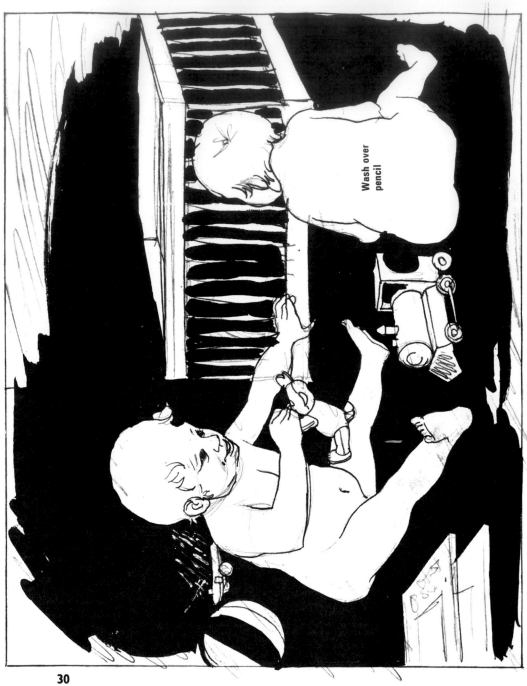

30

Dry Brush

This technique makes use of a medium-grained paper. Dip your brush in the ink, and dry it partially with a cloth or by brushing off the extra ink on any piece of absorbent paper. Then, with your semi-dry brush, *rub* the brush over the drawing. Since your brush has barely enough ink, the little you do have will remain on the uppermost level of the paper's grain, giving it an

Dry brush used in spots as shading. Note large area of white space.

irregularly shaded effect. Dry brush is seldom used as the only technique in a drawing (although it can be), but rather for shading particular areas.

Scratchboard

Engraving began with blocks of wood out of which, by means of burins or chisels, areas were cut away, leaving others in relief. When the woodblock or woodcut was inked, and a sheet of paper pressed over it, the relief zones of the woodcut left black ink impressions on the paper, and the hollow, empty parts of the block did not touch the paper leaving white sections. This is the same principle used in making metal line cuts, of which we have already spoken.

A woodcut can be imitated. One way is by using scratchboard, a board with a blackened *scratchable* coated surface. Out of the coating of the paper, lines may be carved.

We can make our own type of scratchboard. First, do a careful pencil drawing on a thick paper. Be sure the zones of light and shade are clearly determined. Wash with India ink and brush all those areas which should not remain absolutely white.

Now continue with a knife or razor blade in a holder or preferably a lancet. With this, go along "pulling away" ink—once it is dry, of course—from those zones you feel will benefit from this effect. Use the lancet as though it were a pen, only *opening up whites* instead of painting blacks: you can "open up" all kinds of lines and dots.

Part of the same drawing as on page 30, but rendered in imitation scratchboard.

Another technique consists of covering the entire board in black wash, drawing over this with a white grease pencil—once the India ink is dry—and then "bringing out" the entire drawing with the lancet. This is the "purest" method, but of course it is much more difficult.

Authentic woodcut: Detail of Oda a Lorca by Antonio
Frasconi. Note how closely the imitation scratchboard technique resembles it.

This complete drawing was made with a lancet. The artist scratched out white lines from paper
previously covered with black India ink.

1.

2.

3.

4.

1. First put down your thoughts in pencil. 2. Beans and bag seem best, so arrange layouts. 3. You select the bag, so draw it in line. 4. Try it out with cross-hatching and with brush. 5. Another try with line but letters bolder. 6. Semi-dry brush might be better.

5.

6.

UNA COSA ES EL CAFÉ....Y OTRA EL CAFÉ-CAFÉ UN CAFÉ CUALQUIERA PUEDE HACERSE DE CUALQUIER MANERA. EL CAFÉ-CAFÉ, SÓLO PUEDE HACERSE CON CAFÉ. NADA MÁS QUE CAFÉ....PERO BUEN CAFÉ.

Finally, line seems most effective visually, so the advertisement is completed with the addition of deep brown over the beans. The word CAFÉ in brown in the text ties it together.

Correcting a drawing with white opaque gouache

The corrected art after being opaqued

White Gouache as a Cover-Up

Gouache—or tempera—is a water paint used mostly in the correction of errors. India ink, as you know, cannot be erased. The only solution is to *remove* it (scraping it carefully with a knife) or *cover it up* with white gouache. The second is preferable.

It is therefore advisable to keep a tube or jar of white gouache next to your drawing board. With a brush, dilute a small amount of gouache in water, making a fairly thick mixture. Once the India ink is dry, paint over the detail you want to eliminate. The white gouache will "cover" the India ink, making the detail disappear.

Remember that in graphic art, drawings are not destined to be seen as they come from the drawing board, but reproduced. In printing, in the place where you might leave a stain of white gouache *there will be nothing*, as the photoengraving camera will not reproduce white on white paper.

Naturally, you can also use white gouache to paint details on top of black, something like the technique used to "bring out" whites on the scratchboard, but more easily.

3. Color and Paint

You are probably already acquainted with the theory of color and are well aware that the three primary colors are red, blue and yellow. You probably also know that there are many shades of red, blue and yellow obtainable in paints and in gouache.

Are you also aware that in printing with color ink, the printer uses certain colors called process colors? These can be seen in the color wheel below. The printer's inks which are used for the printing of all pictures in color are magenta for the red, cyan for the blue, and a lemon for the yellow, along with black. By combining these colors and overprinting with transparent inks, the printer is able to match almost any color that an artist can paint. An artist

The printer's color ink wheel. These three primaries plus black are called the process colors.

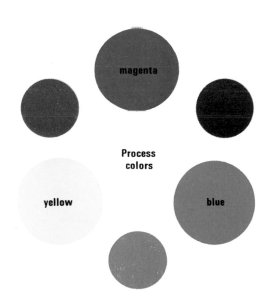

magenta

Process colors

yellow

blue

With the process colors of ink a printer can create combinations that approximate any color.

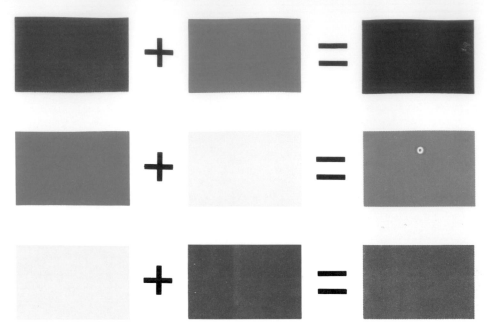

(Top row) Yellow-red plus cyan blue produces a violet.
(Bottom row) Lemon yellow plus yellow-red gives you a pale orange.

painting for reproduction need not concern himself too much with the printer's colors. There are photoengravers (both for letterpress and photolithography) who can color-separate into the four printer's colors any piece of art work that you give them. This is done by a mechanical process and with hand corrections. The color separator uses screens at various angles which convert your work into dots. If you look closely at any printed color picture in a magazine through a magnifying glass, you will see how the dots are arranged.

Actually the graphic artist merely needs to know the same things about color as any other artist.

The red, blue and yellow which are the primary colors in the artist's color wheel are basic in that they cannot be obtained through mixing. The off-reds, off-blues and off-yellows can be obtained by mixing a second primary with the primary. A slight amount of yellow added to red will cause the red to turn toward the orange side. A slight amount of blue mixed with red will tend to create a violet. A mixture of all three primary colors will produce black.

Yellow added to blue, of course, creates green. Therefore we can say that the secondary colors are orange, violet and green. These six are called active colors.

Mixing the three primaries with one another: One primary (blue, for example) with a secondary color composed of two of the other primaries (orange, for example), or one secondary with another secondary, will produce greyed tones: these are the neutral colors.

A knowledge of and ability to handle the colors of paints will be very useful in graphic art work. Naturally, between any two colors of the color wheel—between red and orange, for example—you can have many intermediate colors equally active.

Attributed to the primary colors are the words *hot* and *cold*. Red and yellow are considered hot colors, and blue is considered a cold color. Some reds which contain blue are called cold reds, and other reds are hot. Some blues which contain red are called warm blues.

Visibility test: Pure red is more luminous than when mixed with white or black, as you can see here.

Pure red

Mixed with white

Mixed with black

Against a neutral green background, artist Milton Glaser in this illustration for "Holiday" magazine used pure primaries in some figures and in the flags to create an attractive frame.

Experiments with Color

Many experiments (scientific, psychological, artistic, and commercial), have been performed with color. We are going to examine, briefly, some that will affect you and your work as graphic artists.

Visibility

It has been proved—we have all proved it instinctively—that some colors are more *visible* than others: we see them better, from farther away, and more definitely. Why is one color more "visible" than another? For various reasons:

1. LUMINOSITY. The purer a color, the more luminous it will be. That is to say, a pure red, without any other color mixed in, will always be more visible than a red mixed with white or with black. A color mixed with white or black is a saturated color, with little luminosity. In consequence, *neutral* colors—products of a mixture of three primaries, that, theoretically, lead to black—are less luminous than the *active* colors.

2. HEAT. Since red and yellow are hot, orange will also be hot. Blue is cold, therefore purple and violet—not particularly luminous shades—and green will also be cold. Why? Because both contain blue.

Thus, hot colors are more visible than cold ones, which acquire a blue tone in the distant background. Hot colors, on the contrary, seem to "advance."

This is not mathematical—nothing in art is. For example, a green with a good deal of yellow or a highly reddened violet will appear much warmer. In any case, you must keep in mind the *heat* of the colors in your drawings, since you can create an impression of nearness or distance depending on which you choose.

Hot and cold colors: In the foreground are reds, yellows, oranges —all hot colors. In the middle ground is green, composed of one hot and one cold color. At the back is blue, a cold color. Note how the hot colors "advance" and the cool and cold recede.

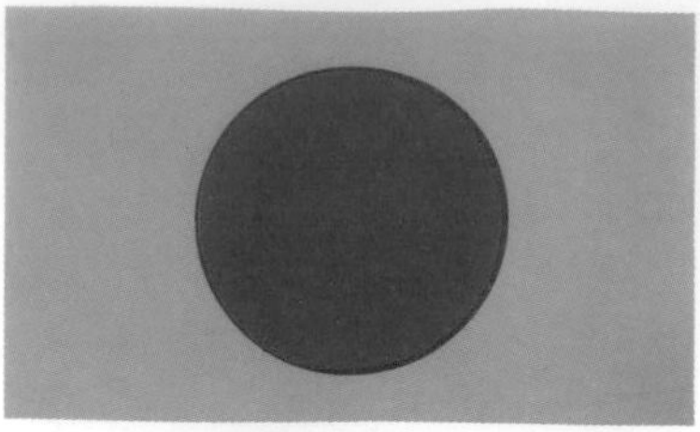

1. Red most visible

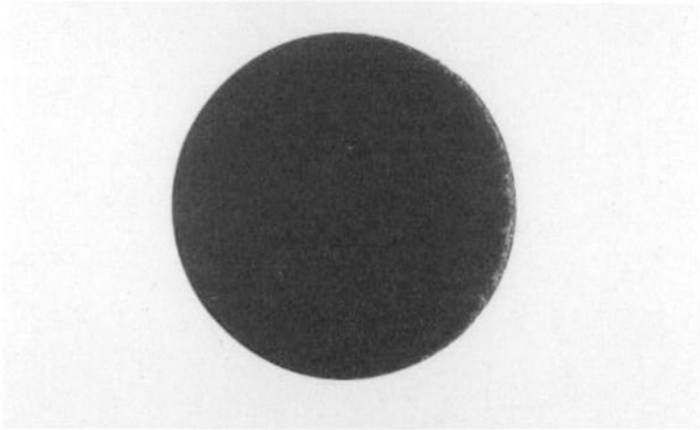

2. Red second most visible

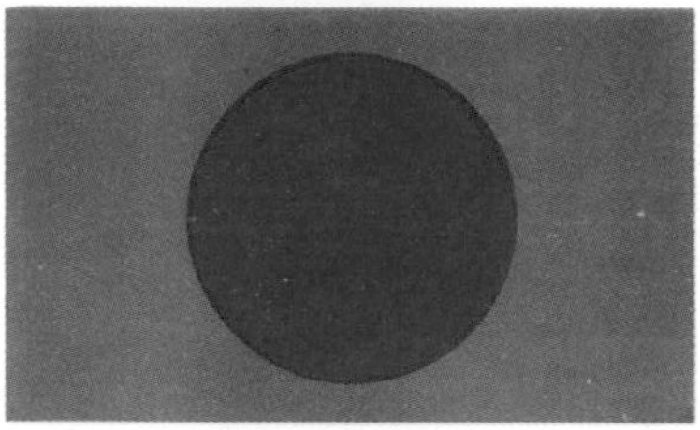

3. Red third most visible

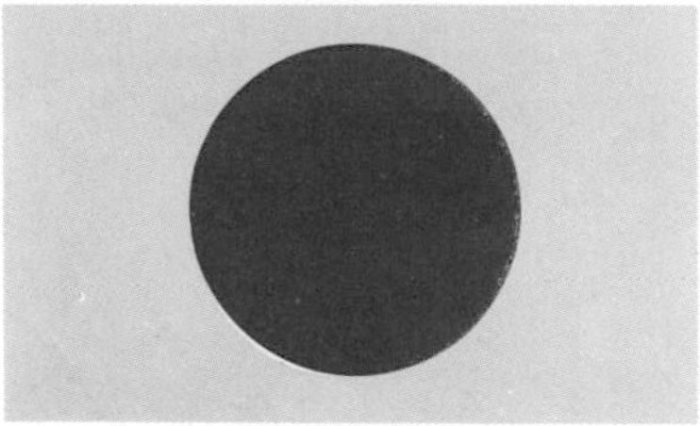

4. Red fourth most visible

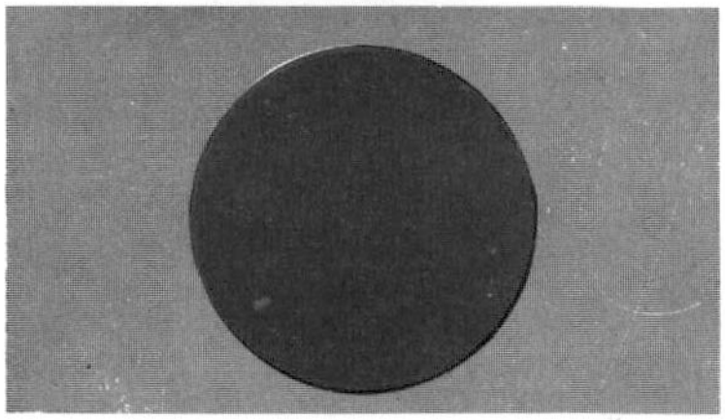

5. Red fifth most visible

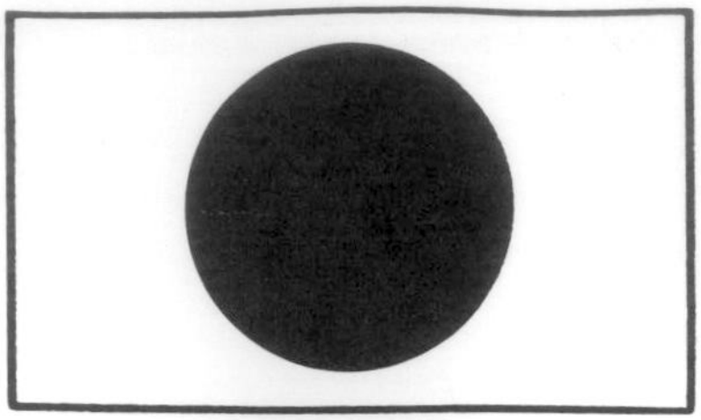

1. Greatest contrast

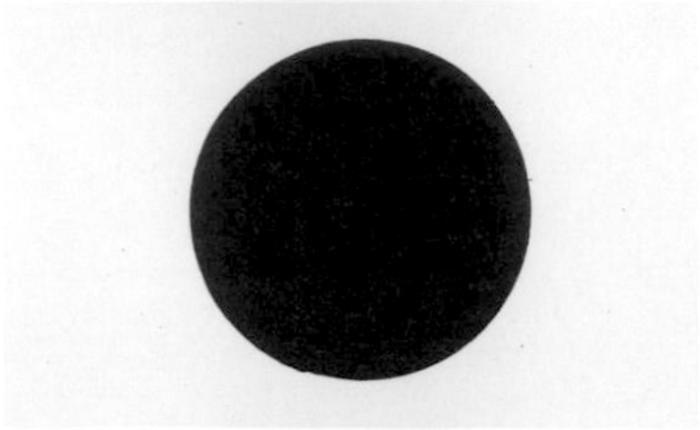

2. Second greatest contrast

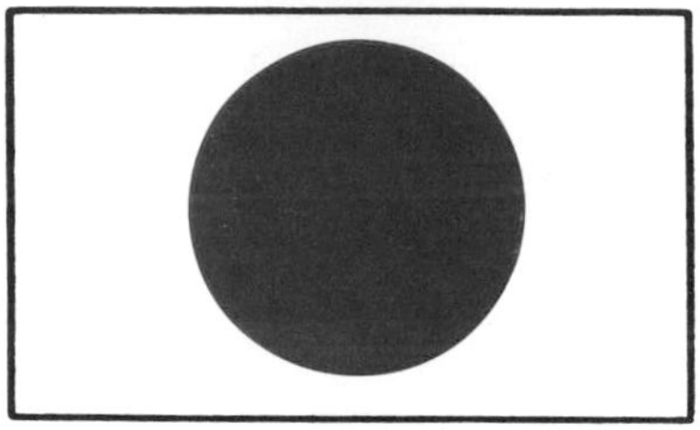

3. Third greatest contrast

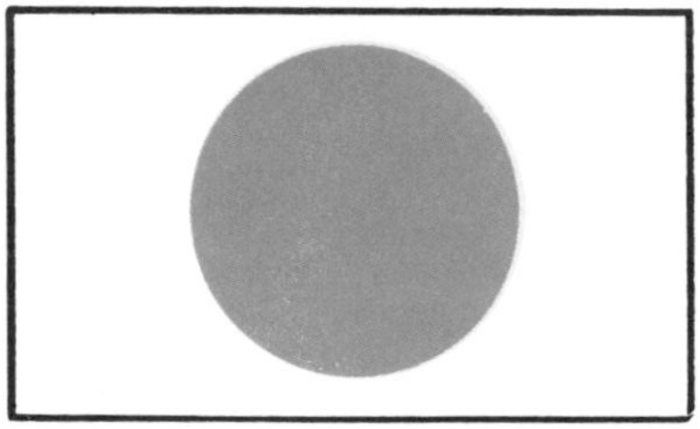

4. Fourth greatest contrast

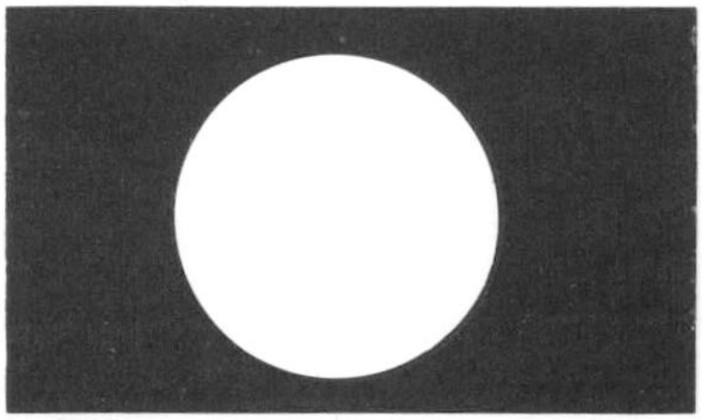

5. Fifth greatest contrast

3. CONTRAST. A color is more or less visible depending on its proximity to another color different from it.

Take red, for example. Its grade of visibility will be different, depending on the color appearing next to it. Here, according to a recent scientific experiment, is the order of visibility of red on five different colors, from maximum to minimum. (See opposite page.)

1. On clear blue (maximum contrast).
2. On lemon yellow.
3. On brownish orange.
4. On a greenish yellow.
5. On a medium grey.

This "law of contrast" is valid, of course, for any color. Here, for example, are the five greatest contrasts established by an English study:

1. Black on white.
2. Black on yellow.
3. Red on white.
4. Green on white.
5. White on red.

And here are the three lowest contrasts:

Green on red.

Red on green.

Black on red.

You should perform your own experiments on contrasts, not always to use the "maximums," but to achieve, in each case, the best solution for your work.

Of course in using contrast, the differences in tone or color are not the only factors; in larger measure, the difference in luminosity is important. A dark red on a dark blue will have a minimum contrast. The same red, on a clear pink (red mixed with a great deal of white), will offer a greater contrast. But the maximum contrast will be achieved by using

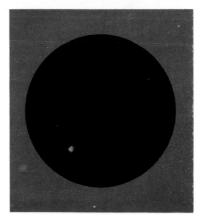

red on clear light blue; then the difference in luminosity will unite the difference in tone.

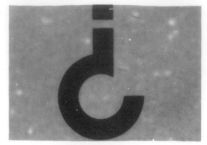

Medium contrast

In these inverted question marks the artist is attracting attention with the unusual position as much as with his contrasting colors.

Maximum contrast

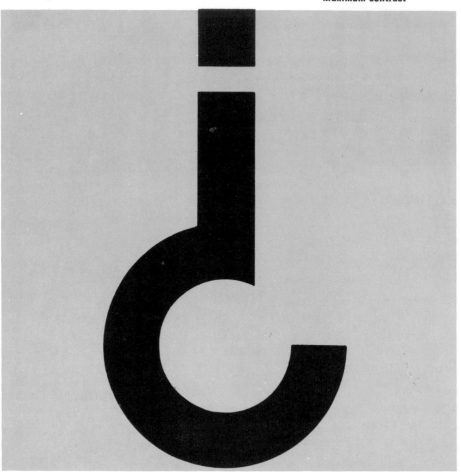

Minimum contrast—but exciting interest in the question

Combination and Harmony

There are many ways to combine colors. Some are *harmonious*, and others are not. What does *harmonious* mean? In music, harmony is the pleasing relationship between two different sounds; in painting it is the good proportion between forms and colors; in the graphic arts, harmony is good proportion and congruity between different colors.

You must understand that in a case like this, where personal taste is a

Monochromatic harmony in a painting in blues alone

factor, it is impossible to define exactly and to give normal rules. Whoever does so commits an error that is unpardonable. In effect, a harmony that is disagreeable to one person may be magnificent to another. Nonetheless, some principles of chromatic harmonies (that is, combinations of colors), are generally accepted as valid:

1. MONOCHROMES consist of paintings in a single color (blue, as in the illustration above) in its different shades. The shades are obtained by the addition of black paint, or white, or black and white, to the basic color. Monochromes, however, require two-color reproductions. The tones of blues are achieved by a halftone engraving process, but the addition of black, even though only used to *darken* the blues in some areas, causes the printer to need two separate engravings and inkings (black and blue).

2. RELATED HARMONIES. If to the previous monochromatic harmony in blue we add a little violet on one side and green throughout, we would have a related or *analogous* harmony, in which all the colors used contain blue.

(Above) Harmonious relationship of blues and greens with a dash of violet. (Left) Harmony through colors that are complementary.

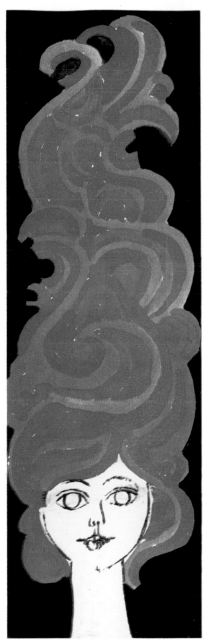

3. COMPLEMENTARIES. Complementary colors are opposites on the color wheel:

blue and orange,
yellow and violet,
red and green.

Harmony can be based upon harmonic pairs, or on a harmonic trio. The primary colors—red, yellow and blue—form one harmonic trio and the secondary colors—orange, green, and violet—form another. Combinations of these trios (harmonies of harmonic trios) can be formed, although with considerable difficulty.

4. NEUTRALS are typical of classical paintings and are simple. Grey is added to all colors, or a pinch to each complementary color. The result is that all the colors are more or less neutral, so that none stands out, and there is no stridency.

Except in special cases, this type of harmony has little application in graphic art. But, what if upon a neutral harmonic back-

Harmonic trio: red, blue and yellow.

ground in which no color dominates, we place, for example, the brand name of the product we are advertising in pure red or pure yellow? Then, the neutrality will have served to enhance what we want to emphasize.

As a last thought, remember that *there is no color that cannot harmonize with another*, as long as the tone and shade are adjusted.

The Color Language of Advertising

The mental associations that certain colors produce have led some artists to establish a color symbolism or color language. This symbolism is rarely scientific. Nevertheless, we should study it briefly, since commercial art is directed at the average person, and for many people the real or supposed significance of each color is important.

GREEN. Communicates freshness, tranquillity, a restful feeling. In some of its tones, a kind of euphoria; in others a vague anguish. It symbolizes hope. It is used in advertisements for mentholated cigarettes, and also for advertising vegetables, oils, etc. As far as *proximity* is concerned, it "conquers" blue and violet, but is conquered by red and yellow.

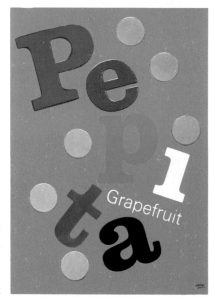

How green conquers blue and violet, but is conquered by reds and yellow.

48

Blue recedes and makes a fine background for hot and bright colors. (By Herbert Leupin.)

No color ever dominates red, which leaps out at the viewer. Mixed with yellow to tones of orange it becomes hottest.

BLUE. The coldest and weakest of the colors, blue "recedes" before the others. The hot colors are made stronger on it: therefore, it is appropriate for backgrounds. If it is surrounded by yellows or reds, it will need a good deal of space or it will be overwhelmed. It symbolizes things like fidelity, honor, faith. In advertising, it is useful for products that inspire cold, such as refrigerators, frozen fish, margarines, etc.

VIOLET. Obtained, as we know, from blue and red, it is colder in proportion to the amount of blue it contains. It can produce discomfort and sadness. It symbolizes luxury and pomp: it is a "religious" color. Appropriate, then, in advertising, for religious articles, parades, etc.

RED. No other color dominates red: this overcomes them all, it "advances" and leaps over the viewer. It is directly associated with fire and blood. Generally it symbolizes a positive, vigorous energy. It can be used for machinery, stoves, kitchens, tonics, etc.

ORANGE. A combination of two hots, orange is the hottest of all the colors. It has a certain vivid, hypnotic force, and penetrates us. When it has little red (pumpkin color), it communicates a vague placidity. As the red increases, violence grows, and it can produce excitement and exhaustion. Even more than red, orange is associated with fire.

YELLOW is a hot color, that communicates light and at the same time a certain blindness. Mixed with orange, it becomes gold and symbolizes wealth and happiness; paled out as lemon it symbolizes dislike. Raw yellow is also considered somewhat gaudy. In advertising, it is appropriate for things related to

light: lamps, polishing products, etc. On the opposite page you can see how an unusual cool feeling is produced by using a warm yellow background in the Coke ad. Below it you can see how yellow becomes stronger when placed over black.

NEUTRAL COLORS. Balance the active colors, allowing the viewer's sight to rest. Grey is preferred in advertising, since it will harmonize with any color. Very light grey, nearly white, is ideal as a background for very pure colors, with less violent an effect than if pure white were used.

BLACK. Any color, placed over black, will appear brighter. At the same time, black, placed over another color, takes advantage of that color's luminosity. Symbolically it is related, of course, to death.

Think of where your ad will be placed—often against a neutral color background. You can then afford to use hot colors.

WHITE "fattens," taking over part of the areas of the colors placed on or around it. Next to any color, it will take on reflections of that color's complementary color; next to blue it takes on a suggestion of orange; next to red, a greenish tinge. White is associated with purity, cleanliness, cold. It symbolizes peace—the white flag—innocence, etc.

Gouache

Just as India ink is the essential element in graphic art drawings, gouache is the basic material of graphic art paintings. For a painter of pictures, a cartoonist, or an illustrator working in pen, knowledge of the gouache technique is helpful. But for a graphic designer or a commercial artist, it is *absolutely necessary*. A commercial artist will use gouache more frequently than any other medium.

A painting in
watercolor.

52

Gouache or tempera, a water paint, is also known as *poster paint*. The very term "poster paint" tells us how important it is to graphic art.

Gouache as we will call it from now on, is an *opaque, covering, and fast-drying paint*. We have seen its power as an opaque cover in white. The fact that it dries so quickly can be an advantage or a disadvantage, according to the situation.

Gouache is composed of ground color pigments, to which ox bile, Arabian gum, and colorless powders have been added for body, as well as glycerine or honey, plus aluminium.

Almost any gouache color, however light and clear it may be, with certain exceptions, can completely block out a darker color underneath. This permits freedom of execution, modifications during the execution that are particularly convenient in commercial art, and final effects that sometimes are the "key" of a poster, illustration or printed advertisement.

The same painting in gouache.

The brilliance or matte quality of gouache colors makes them particularly suitable for photomechanical reproduction. All the colors may be mixed with one another without difficulty and nearly all are stable and resist fading under direct sunlight.

Gouache is obtainable in cakes, tubes and jars. The cakes must be dissolved for commercial art purposes. The tubes are comfortable to use—you have only to squeeze them to obtain the desired quantity of paint—but if it dries inside, there is no remedy. For the artist who works a great deal, the jars are most suitable.

As for brand, choose a jar which indicates on the outside whether the color within can be reproduced with standard printing inks.

The color you need should be removed from the jar on a palette knife or

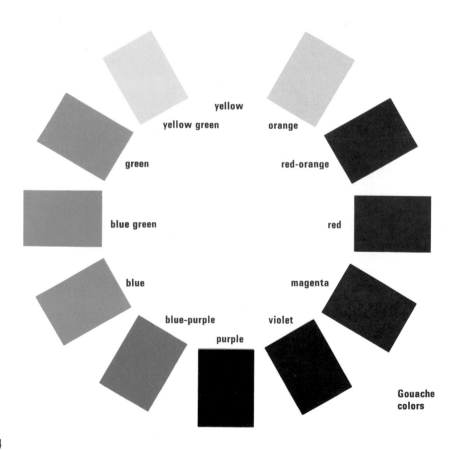

yellow
yellow green   orange
green   red-orange
blue green   red
blue   magenta
blue-purple   violet
purple

Gouache
colors

An excitingly hot painting which stuns the viewer and forces him to look deeper to see the violets in the fish. This effect could not have been achieved except with gouache. Watercolor would have washed out and acrylic or oil paints would not have produced the flat matte finish.

another tool, avoiding the temptation—to which some people succumb—of dipping the brush itself into the jar. By inserting a wet brush in the jar, you dilute the thickness of the paint inside.

Never dip the brush directly into a tube either. Also avoid leaving paint on the inside of the cap; otherwise, the cap will stick to the tube. If, in spite of precautions, the cap does stick, it must be heated with a match; this nearly always works. If it does not, you can submerge the cap and the top of the tube in boiling water, and twist the cap off with the help of a cloth.

After color is removed from the jar with a knife, re-cover the jar immediately. If the color has hardened, it can be resoftened by adding a small amount of boiled water (boiled, not boiling) to the jar, leaving it on top of the paint inside for a few hours, or by adding a damp piece of cotton to the jar.

Materials for Gouache

Brushes, Spatulas and Rollers. Just as for India ink, the best brushes for gouache are sable hair. The rules for their use and care are the same (see page 21).

For certain effects with pure gouache, a palette knife or spatula is needed, as flat as the ordinary bricklayer's spatula. It is very useful to paint planes and contours with it, and quite effective. The knife must be cleaned thoroughly after use, with soap and water, like brushes.

For filling in large masses of flat color, a roller is the surest method of achieving an even background. Rollers are made of rubber or synthetic materials, and can be bought in any art supply store. Their disadvantages? They are absorbent, and waste much paint.

Naturally, all recommended tools can be combined with one another. For example, you can fill in a background with a roller, a figure with a brush or with your fingers, and a second plane of houses with a spatula. In commercial art, there are no academic norms; anything that serves your end is valid.

Don't do this! Remove gouache from the jar with a palette knife. Dipping the brush dilutes the jar's contents.

With gouache on watercolor paper you can obtain a grainy effect to alternate with your smooth solid areas. Keep the gouache thin where you want grains and lay it on thick for the solid areas.

58

PAPERS AND ILLUSTRATION BOARDS. Gouache paper should be fairly heavy, matte finish, sufficiently absorbent, and of medium grain. The very smooth— such as Bristol board—will not do, since it repels water. But poster board, kid finish, will be fine. For certain effects, watercolor paper with a thick grain can be useful.

In any case, our advice is: the thicker the paper, the better. Of course, the heavier the paper, the more expensive it is; but it does not warp, it holds as much color as you may want, and it allows you to add collage materials to it, in addition to making a good impression on the "client."

ACCESSORIES. Any glass will do to hold water. It is best to use several at a time, so that there will always be one with clean water available. To mix colors you can use palette cups of metal or porcelain, or simple concave pieces of crystal or plastic, or even dessert plates. Anything non-absorbent will do.

A cloth and a sponge will also be very useful in cleaning brushes and the work area. The cloth should not contain lint.

VARNISHES AND FIXATIVES. These are not always useful in gouache. In fact at times they are dangerous: they tend to "show up" the mistakes made during

Different utensils for the mixing of gouache colors.

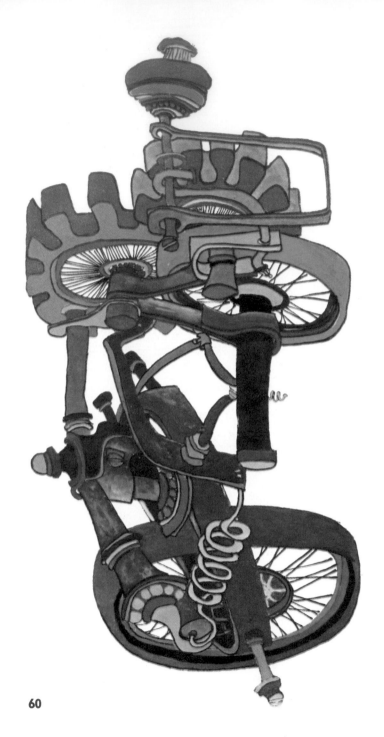

Optimum use of white space as the foundation for a gouache composition. In this painting to attract attention to an advertisement, vivid colors and many strong contrasts have been used.

Tilt your gouache painting up so that when you spray a fixative you do not cause circular stains. Be sure the paint is dry before you begin. Some colors "run."

execution which would have disappeared if the painting had been allowed to dry by itself. It is especially wise to avoid them rigorously if we have used burnt sienna, a color that "bleeds" or runs when varnish is applied on top of it.

If you apply varnish, do so with a broad, flat brush, uniformly, rapidly and softly. You can also varnish with wax: simply rub a piece of candlewax lightly over the surface.

The best way to apply fixative is with an atomizer or spray can. This is a fairly expensive technique, but you have only to push a button and the fixative comes out in vaporized form. Avoid allowing an excessive quantity to fall on the painting: it could cause circular stains. The best plan is to tilt the painting vertically and spray it from a distance in a consistency resembling light rain.

MIXING. Paint with gouache when it is very thick, about the consistency of heavy cream. Add water only to thin it to the desired thickness, never to lighten the color. Gouache must be sufficiently thick to ensure its being opaque, but not so thick that it prevents the brush from moving with it across the painting without difficulty.

To lighten a color in gouache, add *white*, never water. White, moreover, is the most opaque of all the colors, and this is helpful to this technique. The mixtures of colors—red and yellow to make orange, for example—should always be made on the palette or glass plate, never directly on the paper, as

61

For humor, the artist has made the puffs of smoke pink and indicated the heart of the engine in pink too.

you could do with oil or watercolor paints. Add small amounts of each color to the plate, testing until the desired shade is obtained.

Then, when you have a sufficient quantity of the desired color, with the desired fluidity and thickness, try it out with the brush on a piece of paper. Only then begin to paint with it.

EQUALITY OF TONE. It is almost impossible to achieve the same tone twice in gouache mixtures. And it is *totally* impossible to "dovetail" two fragments of gouache paint of the same tone with the hope that they will "not be noticed." They will invariably be noticed.

The secret? As just noted previously: prepare a sufficient quantity of color. And always work *wet*. While painting, while the gouache is still wet, it will seem that there are discrepancies in tone. Do not be frightened. These inequalities will disappear in the drying, after which the uniformity will be absolute.

But take care. If you have permitted yourself even the tiniest correction, the most infinitesimal retouch on the dry or semi-dry gouache, you are lost. Fatally, the retouch will be noticeable. Consequently, follow this invariable rule: *in tempera, everything wet, never dry, if we want equality of tone.*

Always keep a glass of clean water handy. Mix gouache in palette cups, not on the paper. Be certain to mix a sufficient quantity of a color, because no two batches are ever exact matches.

APPLYING TONES. In gouache, unlike watercolor, the logical procedure is to paint the dark zones first, then the medium, and last the lights, such as the white highlights. But this is not an absolute rule.

In any case, there is no special problem, since you are working with flat coats, in areas of color that do not blend with others. It is sufficient, then, to apply the touches you wish over previous coats.

WORK QUICKLY. This is only necessary when you want a large mass—a background, for example—of a uniform tone. In all other cases, you must wait (not too long, since gouache is fast-drying) until one color is dry before applying another on top of it.

BLENDING COLORS. You might want to blend one color with another for a special effect. This can be achieved with bands of color that grow progressively lighter, joined together or not. If you decide to unite them, you must work extremely quickly, passing the wet brush—dampened in clean water—on top of the lines between one band and the next.

You can also blend gouache by putting one color at one end and another at the opposite extreme, and then *working wet* to unite them quickly and softly, progressively with fluidity. Be sure to work as quickly as possible.

A method that does not require quick work is this: First paint in the lightest color of the two to be blended. Let this dry, then, with the brush lightly dipped in the other color, apply touches of the second color to the first, with strokes progressively more spaced out, finer or thicker, according to the desired effect.

Of course, you can also begin by painting the dark color first, and once this is dry, begin adding touches of the lighter color.

For uniform coverage, work from the top down. Work quickly.

When you need a second coat to cover, wait until the first coat is dry, then paint quickly and no lines will show.

CORRECTING ERRORS. To correct in gouache is dangerous. In the first place, the work must be completely dry, and the entire zone of color must be corrected. You must never "patch" a tone, since it will unavoidably remain a patch. It is not wise to overpaint any single area, since the paper may resist. And, of course, the eraser is completely unsuitable for the correction of errors in gouache: the only thing an eraser will produce is a series of unequal shines.

Professional "Secrets"

In each technique, there are little "tricks" that help you to achieve unusual results. They are the "secrets" of the professional, that produce admiration in the beginner. They are recourses—the word "trick" is excessive and not really appropriate.

Professional recourses can be used by anyone familiar with them. The idea is not to use a recourse mechanically, but to investigate each potential technique constantly. Here are some of the most useful recourses that the gouache technique permits:

DRY BRUSH. This recourse—very useful in gouache—is the same as was discussed in the chapter on penline techniques (see page 31).

Blending

Note the circle left in an attempt to correct by overprinting

Blending red at one end with black at the other

Here we see different gradations and mixtures of colors: gradations of violet for borders, in the lantern; dry brush, in the picture in the background; blended in water, in the flowers; running color, in the vase; brushing with thick color over a previous coating, on the apple; lighter shade over a layer of a darker shade of the same color, in the candelabra. Finally, progression from yellow to violet, by means of stripes.

WET-ON-WET. When you apply one color, in extremely liquid mixture, on top of another that is not yet completely dry, the effects are always a bit unpredictable. Take advantage of the technique, but be aware of the hazards that this does present. The results—somewhat resembling watercolor—can often be excellent.

WAX RESIST. If you rub the surface of the paper with candlewax before painting, the gouache will adhere less, and part of it can be removed later on with a knife. You can also "draw" with the candle stub; When you paint over this later with gouache the color will barely adhere to where you made the wax "drawing," so these lines will appear white, on a background of color.

If you rub the wax over a background already painted in a certain color, then paint over this later on, the color will adhere only to those areas not previously waxed; in these areas the background color will remain, with an irregular appearance.

SCRATCHING. Scraped areas can be attractive. Use the handle of the paint brush on wet gouache. On dry gouache, use the knife technique explained on page 31 in regard to line drawing.

On a dry background of the desired color, rub wax uniformly. Then remove part of the wax by scratching or scraping it. When you subsequently paint a contrasting color on this scratched waxy surface, the new paint will not "take," and the background color will show.

SPATTER. Wetting a brush of any sort (an old toothbrush, perhaps) in very diluted gouache and flicking it with a razor blade in the direction of the paper produces a "spattered" color, that falls on the paper like fine, uneven rain.

A variation of this technique consists of placing a fine or coarse metallic screening (an

Wet-on-wet gouache

Wax resist background

When gouache is completely dry, scraping becomes difficult

The effect of sponging in different colors over a dry gouache background

old window screen or chicken wire, perhaps) at some distance above the paper and rubbing a gouache-loaded brush over it. The "spattering" will be less fine in this case: it will more or less follow the pattern of the screening.

Sponge. Dipping a small sponge in paint and then pressing it on the work will create irregular backgrounds of great variety, depending on the porosity of the sponge and how much paint it is carrying.

Stencil. This technique is to protect a pre-determined area from paint through laying down or pasting on a paper stencil. It is then easy to paint around it. When the stencil is removed the protected area remains white. Stencils are especially useful to protect given areas when using the spatter technique.

Rubbings. This is painting, but similar to printing. It is done by dipping almost anything in paint—pieces of cloth, vegetable leaves, flowers—and pressing one side of the wet object onto the paper. The relief areas of the paint-dipped object will *print* on the paper or board.

The white mottle in the red is obtained by pressing a paint-soaked cloth onto the paper

The white semicircle was preserved by a white stencil

Other Paints

WATERCOLOR dries as fast as gouache, but is transparent. Therefore, you must paint from light to dark tones. To lighten colors, water, not white paint, must be used. Since it is not opaque and therefore does not "cover," it is impossible to correct errors.

Watercolor is most appropriate for illustrations—it gives a spontaneous and fresh appearance. It would not be appropriate, for example, to design a brochure, a poster, or an advertisement *completely* in watercolor; but you could use watercolor in a *part* of a brochure, poster, or advertisement.

OIL PAINT. Like gouache, this is a "covering" paint. And oils are more "flexible." Disadvantages? Oil paints dry slowly. But this can be remedied by adding a cobalt drier to the colors. Oil, inappropriate for flat or matte colors, would be, on the other hand, necessary for advertisements or posters which should have a "pictorial" quality.

Acrylic painting that looks like watercolor

ACRYLIC PAINTS. Acrylic paints can be used just like oils, by adding a small amount of water; or just like watercolors, by diluting them with a good deal of water. They can be transparent or opaque, according to need. They do not dry as slowly as oil (an advantage), but do take a little longer to dry than gouache (another advantage). What are their disadvantages, then? For one, realistically, their cost. A tube of acrylic paint costs much more than gouache or oil.

69

4. Advertising Recourses

We have already noted that the commercial artist has a series of "recourses" available to him, recourses without apparent relationship to drawing and painting. For this reason it is preferable to call the commercial artist a graphic artist. Here are some of the most useful and well known recourses of the graphic artist:

Self-Adhering Letters

These are something like decals, and they are available in shops that cater to the artist. The major part of your lettering requirements will be resolved with these self-adhering (or rub-on) letters. A wide variety of lettered alphabets are available.

Handling these letters is quite simple. You simply apply pressure to the letter—with a round-end stylus or an unfilled mechanical pen, for example—without pressing too hard. The plastic covering is then lifted and the letter has been "printed" on the paper. In case of a mistake, you can paste a piece of special self-adhesive tape over the incorrect letter and rub the correction tape with the mechanical pen. Then when you pull it up, the wrong letter will adhere to the tape and lift off.

ABCDEF abc
440 24pt/d ■ GER/SCA/ESP

ABCDEFG abcd
441 20pt/d ■ ENG/GER/FRA/SCA/ESP

ABCDEFGHIJ abcde
442 16pt/d ■ ENG/GER/FRA/SCA/ESP

ABCDEFGHIJK abcdef
443 14pt/d ■ GER

ABCDEFGHIJKLM abcdefghi
444 12pt/d ■ GER

ABCDEFGHIJKLMNOP abcdefghij
445 10pt/d ■ GER

Folio Medium Extended

ABC
447 60pt/d ■□ GER

abc
448 60pt/d □□ GER

ABCD
449 48pt/d ■□ ENG/GER/FRA/SCA/ESP

abcd

Rub-on lettering is a great time-saver and a boon to graphic artists who need large-size letters. (Left photo) Place the sheet in position and press down firmly on the letter to be "printed." (Right photo) Lift the sheet and the letter remains. Many sizes and styles of type are available.

ABCD
462 48pt/d ☐☐ ENG/GER/FRA/SCA/ESP

abcde
463 48pt/d ☐☐ ENG/GER/FRA/SCA/ESP

ABC ab
464 36pt/d ☐ ENG/GER/FRA/SCA/ESP

ABCDEab
465 28pt/d ENG/FRA/SCA/ESP

ABCDE abc
466 24pt/d GER/SCA/ESP

ABCDEF abc
467 20pt/d ENG/GER/FRA/SCA/ESP

ABCDEFGHIabcd
468 16pt/d ENG/GER/FRA/SCA/ESP

ABCDEFGHIJ abcde
469 14pt/d GER

ABCDEFGHIJKL abcdefg
470 12pt/d GER

ABCDEFGHIJKLMN abcdefgh
471 10pt/d GER

Folio Bold Condensed

ABCDE

Folio Extra Bold

ABCD
484 48pt/d ☐ GER

abcd
485 48pt/d ☐☐ GER

ABCDa
486 36pt/d GER/SCA/ESP

ABCDEab
487 28pt/d ENG/FRA/SCA/ESP

ABCDEFab
488 24pt/d GER/SCA/ESP

ABCDEFG abc
489 20pt/d ENG/FRA/SCA/ESP

Futura Medium

A
109 39mm ☐② ENG/GER/SCA

Instead of attempting to paint large flat colored areas, use cut-outs and paste them on in layers.

Collage

Scissors and glue will frequently be of more use to you than brushes or ink. With imagination, anything can be cut out and pasted down to form a magnificent conception for a poster or advertisement: photographs, pieces of cloth, newspaper clippings, etc. The idea is, of course, to "compose" or combine these cutouts to achieve two ends: a certain aesthetic beauty, as well as the utilitarian, or functional, purpose of the product being advertised.

Laminating with Colored Papers

This is an extension of a technique we discussed earlier. In art supply shops you can find papers, glossy or matte, thick or thin, of various colors. Often, for a large area of color—on a poster, for example—it is more practical to paste a colored paper cut to the desired shape on a white paper than to take the time to paint the area with gouache.

Just like gouache, proceed with these colored papers in flat layers or laminations: on a brown cutout—a tree-trunk—you might superimpose green cutouts for the leaves, and on these, red cutouts for the fruits. There are no limits to this technique.

Various Adhesive Shapes

In the case of the tiny red cutouts for the fruits, save yourself the bother of using scissors and paste. There are many shapes—circles of various diameters, rectangles, squares—in many standard colors, already gummed on the back,

A sheet of adhesive shapes

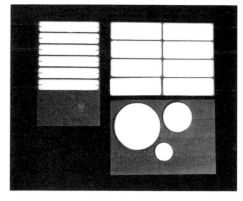

(Left) An adhesive sheet of dots, called a Benday pattern, has been laid over an ink drawing.

Part of a jacket for a mathematics book on which adhesive shapes have been used

available in art supply shops. Remove the protective paper from the gummed side and apply the shapes by pressure. If you use white shapes, they can first be painted with the exact color you want.

For a book jacket or a poster filled with tiny circles of color, there can be no doubt that the colored adhesive shapes will save you a great deal of work. And not only that: they will give the work a uniformity very difficult to attain in any other manner.

Shading

Preprinted lines or dots on acetate can be purchased. These come in various intensities and sizes, to produce a more or less dark impression of grey for shaded areas.

Acetate sheets have to some extent been replaced by self-adhesives. Previously you had to cut the exact area and glue it on or over the work as an overlay. With the self-adhesives you just press on, as with the letterset alphabets already described.

There is also a chemically treated paper upon which you can draw in the usual fashion. Then later, you dip a brush in a special liquid that comes with the paper and wash over the areas that you wish to grey. A fine-screen dot shadow "appears."

Last, there is the Benday screen which the photoengraver or lithographer creates. Do not try to apply it yourself. Simply indicate to the photoengraver where you want him to lay it. You need only to rule out those areas with blue pencil, and he will take care of the rest.

How to indicate on your art where you want a mechanical Benday dot screen laid by the photoengraver. (Top right) The original penline drawing. (Middle) Blue pencilling indicates area. (Lower right) The finished art with the shading in place.

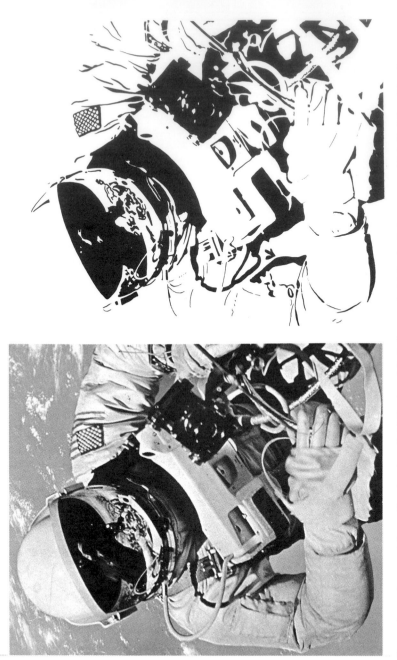

Converting a photograph into a line drawing: (Left) On the original photograph, ink in the darkest tones with India ink and brush or pen. Strengthen the intermediate folds and lines that you want to retain—as shown here. (Right) The photograph has been dipped in an emulsion (see page 77) and only black and whites are left. The half tones have disappeared.

Printed Letters

When an advertisement will carry a great many letters, for example, instead of using rub-on type it would be preferable to send the copy—if the client agrees—to a typesetter or to the publication to be typeset. It will be sufficient to indicate to him your choice of typeface from a specimen type book, and the width. Then, with the proof printed on good coated reproduction paper, you can cut and paste up the type as you want it to appear.

We can also use decorative printed letters, combining them with type. These can be obtained in rub-on type or you can draw them or trace them out of a type sample book.

Photographs in Line

There are two methods to convert a photograph into a "penline" print. One of these is done in a photographic laboratory, and we cannot discuss it here, in spite of the fact that it is the better method. The second method is by hand.

It is very simple. Take a photograph—pale if possible—and go over its darkest parts with India ink, using a brush or a pen. Do not touch the light zones: the idea is to make a selection of black and white zones, on purpose.

Then submerge the photograph in the following mixture: four or five tablespoons of water, a teaspoon of hyposulphite of soda (thiosulphate), and a teaspoon of iron cyanid. In just a moment the photographic emulsion will have disappeared, leaving only the India ink: you will have what resembles a line drawing.

5. Posters and Devices

For many, the poster *is* commercial art. In any case, it is the advertising medium with the most tradition and prestige, the medium that first "catches the eye" because of its size, which may range from 8 inches up to 30 feet, as on a billboard. Of course, posters offer the most opportunities for creativity. A good proof of its importance in advertising is that, as we already know, gouache colors are called poster colors.

Multiple production of posters of large size were not possible before the "invention" of printing. But the golden age of the poster came in the 19th century, with the increased usage of lithography, a process that made the printing of posters in different colors economically possible.

(Left) An anti-war poster by Brangwyn. (Right) Poster by the Beggarstatt Brothers.

Poster by the most famous
of all poster artists,
Henri de Toulouse-Lautrec.

Poster
by Kurt
Wirth

Styles and Techniques

There are many kinds of posters. It is not
necessarily true that one is better than
another, but in each case you must search
for the most appropriate resolution to your
poster problem. For this reason, it is a good
idea to have a quick look at the principal
styles and techniques of the poster.

On an aerial photograph, the artist has superimposed a studio photograph and artwork with hand lettering for a 1910 aviation conference.

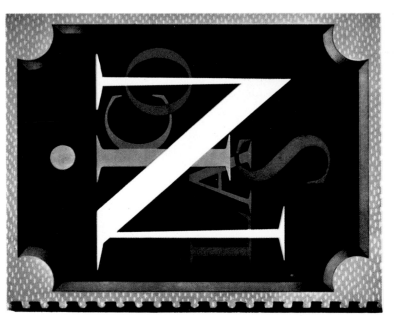

An abstract poster with jumbled lettering—all in different sizes and colors—that holds your attention. (By A. M. Cassandre.)

ABSTRACT MOTIFS. In this kind of poster there is nothing objective or figurative. There are no bottles, nor bulls, nor trains—only shapes of color. Graphic abstraction is less customary in the poster than in other commercial art forms. Perhaps this is because the poster is not "seen;" it is "glanced at" in passing. The graphic idea must be conveyed *immediately*.

There are, notwithstanding, plastic themes (architecture, etc.), or subjects difficult to portray symbolically (conventions, pharmaceutical products, etc.), that lend themselves perfectly well to an abstract poster treatment. And even more frequently artists use an abstract composition "finished" with a small figurative motif.

PHOTOGRAPHY. This is much used in the present-day poster, particularly in travel posters. Our problem will consist, sometimes, of selecting the most appropriate photograph, and, always, of deciding where it will be cropped, where the letters or type will be placed, selecting the colors and the typeface, etc.

PHOTOMONTAGES. These offer great possibilities, if the artist has imagination. The technique consists of cutting, pasting and combining photographs and letters in the best possible fashion. If you are not very sure of the result, you can "test" the effects by sketching them first on a separate piece of paper. You must be careful to select the best-quality photographs possible.

Humorous treatment for a cognac ad in a poster by Paul Degen.

Abstract with a star in a poster by Bronislaw Zelek for the fifth anniversary of the Polish Communist Revolution.

ZSRR-awangardą pokoju, wolności i postępu

(Top left) A geometric poster with a central object—an envelope—created for the Netherlands post office. (Above) Humor attracts attention in this poster by Celestino Piatti. (Lower left) Announcing a modern cinema. By Waldemar Swierzy. (Below) A cartoon poster of sorts by Ziraldo Pinto.

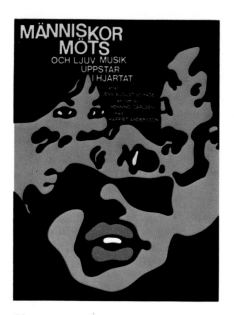

"ANTIQUED" EFFECTS. You can intentionally use an object or an old-fashioned style in a modern poster: this would be a deliberate antiqued effect. You can draw in the style of a given era, or blow up photographically an authentic drawing of that age. There are themes, such as antique car races, that are very appropriate for this type of poster.

GEOMETRIC FORMS. These are nearly always extremely effective, if the colors and the shapes have been well selected. Serene geometric shapes never tire, and they are very appropriate for themes like books or construction, for example.

THE CARTOON. The cartoon—an effective poster if it is good—requires a specialist. If you are not a specialist in the drawing of cartoons, limit yourself to styling the type for and pasting up the poster, leaving the cartoon for a specialist.

REALISM. Painted "realism" has fallen into disuse, since the color photograph has taken its place. But a poster with a stylized, realistic pictorial quality, executed in broad brush-strokes, still has possibilities.

LETTERS AND VARIED ELEMENTS. We have already seen, when discussing self-adhesive letters, that letters by themselves constitute a decorative element. Letters alone can produce excellent posters, if they are handled properly. You can cut them, paste them, broaden them, and place them on the poster in many ways. (See illustration on page 80.)

We can say the same of any other element: antique engravings, children's drawings,

The bottle in the photograph distorts the lettering behind it, but only enough to attract attention. By Herbert Leupin.

Letters form a poster for a book publisher.

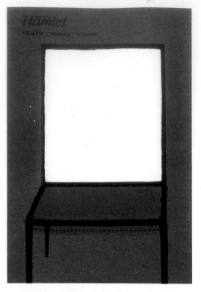

musical scoring paper, bits of cloth, reproductions of paintings, etc. You can use all of these elements in the poster. A poster artist is not an artist who necessarily paints or draws well; a poster artist is one who distributes things well in the space of the poster.

In general, it is not wise to have the name of the product at the head of the poster; the "title" should not be too large; a photograph or a cartoon are the most effective visually; long pictorial vistas should be avoided; it is better to present a detail than a whole form; contrasts of cold or light colors are not usually effective; and, above all, that a poster cannot announce two things at the same time.

Simple composition for a theatrical poster by Henryk Tomaszewski.

Gouache painting for a travel poster by Donald Brun.

Subjects

The principal subjects for posters—apart from the traditional product or service advertising—could be said to be these:

- Tourism, conventions and fairs.
- The cinema.
- The theatre and music.
- Sports events.
- Political posters.
- "Image" or public relations posters.

Warm colors for a warm country in a poster by Claus Knezy.

A photograph is the most visually effective billboard.

For each subject—and, within these, in each specific case—apply the style and technique that seem most suitable to you. In the travel poster, for example, resort nearly always to the photograph, while the sports poster has a very special tradition.

The cinema, theatre and music, on the other hand, may be treated in very different ways, using photograph or cartoon, and ranging from abstract motifs to realism to typography. But, above all, the elements—the movie camera, the film itself, the theatre's masks of comedy and tragedy, musical notes—offer a rich graphic symbolism upon which to draw in your posters.

Political posters should be directed to all the citizens entitled to vote. They should, therefore, call attention to the candidate or party strongly, and be easily understood by anyone.

"Image" or public relations posters are used by commercial enterprises to give their products a certain artistic flair, cultural or human. Frequently the poster itself will not have any direct relationship to the product; instead it will

A billboard can be treated as just a large poster.

deal with a more or less important theme of general interest. The fact that they are called "image" posters is a clue to their distinguished refined style, which is meant to give the impression that the firm commissioning the poster has "class."

The pale blue background sets off a humorous situation.

1.

2.

3.

4.

1. Trademarks composed of letters only. 2. Letters arranged within designed spaces. 3. Graphic symbol related to the service (aviation). 4. Free graphics, without direct symbolic relationship to the product.

Brand Names and Trademarks

Commercial artists regard a brand name and its trademark as the visual device or symbol of a product or service.

Since earliest times, brands served to distinguish one thing from others similar to it: Brands have marked cattle for as long as men had cattle. In the Middle Ages, each knight had his "coat-of-arms," which was something like his trademark. Religions also adopted graphic symbols (the cross), as later the professions—and later political ideologies—did.

Specifically commercial trademarks had their origin in posters and signs that needed instant recognition. Watermarks and hallmarks were the symbols used by paper manufacturers and porcelain and pottery makers to distinguish their products from the competition.

Since their very origin, trademarks have demanded to be simplified forms. All graphic symbols have to be reproduced by simple methods: by branding irons, in weaves, on borders, gummed or wax seals, sealing-wax molds, woodcuts, or cut metal. This made it imperative that the forms themselves should also be simple, and easy to reproduce.

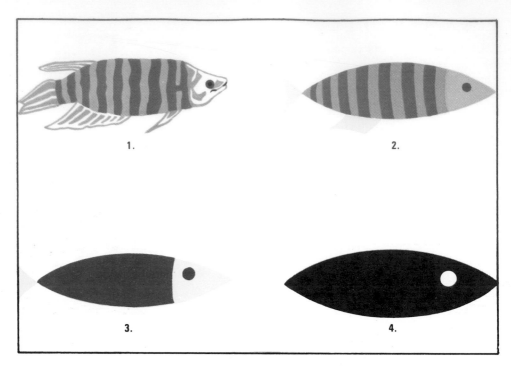

The process of simplification. (1) A real brilliantly colored fish. (2) Simplified fish usable for four-color lithography. (3) Simplified fish down to two colors. (4) Abstracted to its ultimate, the fish is now a single-color trademark.

When new methods of reproduction, such as photolithography, were perfected, the trademarks became more complicated. But today we have nevertheless returned to the simple, the functional, the synthesis. A trademark must be seen and recognized easily, and it must be reproducible by any method.

VISUAL EFFECTIVENESS. A trademark should be visually effective. To achieve this it should:

1. *Affect the memory.* It must be "recorded" easily and be distinguishable from any other trademark.

2. *Relate to the thing it advertises.* It must clearly show that the trademark refers to a specific product.

3. *Possess graphic beauty.* It must have, in addition to the power to call the

viewer's attention to it, enough of a pleasing quality to make people remember it pleasantly.

A trademark is something that may be used forever. It should not go out of style. It should not, therefore, follow too closely the graphic fads of the moment, but seek instead a certain classic quality, which is achieved, always, only through *synthesis*.

A trademark can, from the graphic point of view, be: (a) The name of the product; (b) a drawing that symbolizes the product in some fashion; (c) an attractive, but not symbolic, graphic presentation; (d) the name, plus the drawing, symbolic or not.

The Advertisement

The format of an advertisement depends upon the number of a given publications' columns, their width and their height. Given the customary format of daily newspapers and magazines they will nearly always be rectangular—vertical or horizontal—and seldom square. No matter what size you work in the advertisement has to fit in one, two or three columns, by width, and proportional height; or occupy an entire page, half page, quarter page or eighth page. The half page, as well as the quarter or the eighth, can be vertical or horizontal.

Advertisements in newspapers are generally in black and white; they are generally line cuts or coarse screen halftones and you should execute them, therefore, in the line and cross-hatch technique or with Benday screens. Magazine advertisements in black and white, on the other hand—since they are usually printed by letterpress (photoengraving) or photo-offset lithography—can be prepared with pen or gouache, whichever is desired. If the advertisements are to appear in color, the custom is to use the gouache technique in the manner used for the preparation of posters.

6. Creativity in Graphic Art and Advertising

These pages have not been more than a timid and modest look at the fabulous, broad world of graphic art. In spite of this, you may have been able to learn something of the two essential problems of commercial art: *technique* and *creativity*.

Perhaps you have also understood another basic fundamental: the certainty that the two problems are intimately linked. If you have mastered technique, but lack creative ideas, you will be able to do little in the field of graphic art (second-rate work, in the majority of cases). In the same fashion, despite a fund of ideas, you will not be able to accomplish important work without a firm knowledge of techniques that will allow you to execute them well.

To know what procedure, what style, what medium, what tool to use is helpful in any given advertisement, poster, or brochure; to know all this is to know *technique*, but it also begins to be *creativity*.

Poets can speak of the muses that inspire their creations. But in the field of graphic art such romantic language is out of place. Some days are more inspiring than others, but creativity in general is composed of patience, experience and perseverance. And IMAGINATION, it goes without saying.

To describe the mechanics of creativity is little short of impossible. Its stages nearly always evolve unconsciously at the hour and minute of the specific work. We can, however, attempt to systematize. Take, for example, a newspaper advertisement. What would the stages of the creative process be?

Simplified, they would be these:
1. A series of sketches for ideas.
2. Selection of the best ideas.

3. Organization of the ideas selected in proportion to the final space (chosen by us or assigned).

4. Selection of the most appropriate style (line, shaded line, wash, dry brush, etc.).

5. A pencil sketch.

6. Execution and completion of the final art.

In some cases there can be additional steps:

7. Adaptation of the advertisement to other formats.

If you are dealing with a poster advertisement, as opposed to a newspaper advertisement, the two first steps will not differ essentially, nor will the third. You would then follow these steps:

4. Various color sketches (harmonizing).

5. Selection of the best harmony.

6. Selection of the appropriate style or technique (smooth, flat colors, pictorial style, collage, etc.).

7. Pencil sketch.

8. Execution and completion of the final art.

(Left) A fantastic poster in the abstract, purely imaginary but based perhaps on a Rorschach ink-blot test. (Right) For an Alexander Nevsky film, the symbols of this poster are completely relevant.

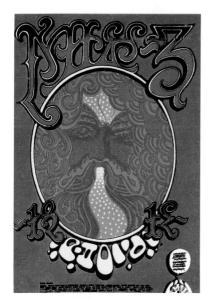

1.

2.

1. Sketch ideas in pencil. 2. Enlarged sketch of selected idea.

3.

3. Try-outs for color harmony.
4. Brush interpretation. 5. Color variation. 6. Simple color.

4.

5.

6.

Final advertisement. The solid red seems most attractive and simplest too. The type looks best typeset.

Index